# A Mindful Existence

## The planning guide for the entrepreneur

## Creating your world of peace

by

# Ellice Darien

# A Mindful Existence

Copyright © 2017 Ellice Darien

All rights reserved.

ISBN: **1541015940**
ISBN-13:978-1541015944

# A Mindful Existence

## DEDICATION

To the probation officer who said to me "Never get in a position where others control you."

## CONTENTS

    Acknowledgments    i

1. My World    1
2. Your World
3. Recognizing Our Gifts
4. Procrastination
5. Stepping Out On Faith
6. Smarter Goals
7. Planning

# A Mindful Existence

### ACKNOWLEDGMENTS

Thanks everyone who positively put up with me

# Chapter 1: My World

Ok, I decided to write a book because I would always say "If I wrote this stuff in a book nobody would believe me!" Well, I decided to write one, but not only a book of memories or how to overcome obstacles, but also a guide to control. See, with a lot of my downfalls there was no preparation, no research, or guidance.

I also believe that I don't have to write a book the size of war and peace, and I can tell you that I don't have time to write one as well as you probably don't have time to read one. Time is a miserable lady.

## BACKGROUND

I can start with: I was born in Brooklyn; parents both from Jamaica West Indies. I was raised by my father. I went to school. I married young; my ex husband (a bum) and I had babies. The rest the same as most of you.

## SOME OF MY JOBS (and the hustles)

I've been a Retail person. Assistant sales manager, Telemarketer, Inside sales Rep, Account Executive, Sales Trainer, Project Coordinator, Beautician (owned a salon), Home Health Aide, Certified Nurses Aide, Nurse, Entrepreneur owner of ByDarien and Darien Essentials.

In most of these jobs someone else was in control. I hated it. Now please don't get me wrong; I believe that we all have a role and a dream, and not everyone is an entrepreneur, but I always wanted to be Alexis Carrington ~ remember that show Dynasty ( young ones google it). So ... I was never satisfied; I always felt as if I wasn't the best at any of these except the latter. I hated doing hair, but I loved the marketing of the salon, the sales, the adrenaline, the money.

## IT TOOK ABOUT 48 YEARS

It took that long to clean my room as a child, and as an adult I could never manage my home, I could never get it together; my life was always too busy ...the chaos, the disappointments, the heartbreaks, the self-blame, etc. However, if I had just learned to physically take control and mentally become efficient _____. And it's always a work in progress.

I had a time when I had lost control of everything. I never had great luck, but this stuff ~ I lost our home ; My business was failing; my elderly mother needed increased attention. Which causes some family to turn against me On top of that we would have cars that either died or got repossessed. even mechanical things would die. I was in the twilight Zone.

It seemed as if there wasn't a happy moment until my precious grandson was born, then my daughter called , my grandson was born with SMA1 (spinal muscular atrophy) is a disease that robs people of physical strength by affecting the motor nerve cells in the spinal cord, taking away the ability to walk, eat, or breathe. It is the number one genetic cause of death for infants. SMA is caused by a mutation in the survival motor neuron gene 1 (SMN1). (until now those babies don't live to see their 2nd year).

Then as a mother and a grand mom I had to and still had to deal with the family, my precious daughter who of course I have always been proud of but no words to describe the pride I feel when seeing her strength and love for my grandson
What else? Well, there was more ~ I'm keeping it short remember. However, I always had a knack of having very great friends, true gems. I always thought I had the key to picking them, and I cover that in this book also.

Then it happened, one day we got a new apartment, and I cleaned and organized, and cleaned and cleaned again. I knew where everything was; where it belonged. A tip from a friend was to organize the way you think. In other words the supermarket tries to organize the aisles the way you cook. The Sugar with the flour and the salt etc.. my first start to gaining control

Now I had to try to put this to my business, because I didn't know anything about my own Business, I realized that as I was living thru this hard time, there were no systems, I didn't know my financial (my numbers) I did not even have products when any emergency happened, my business could not run itself and no one could take over few a few days because there was nothing written down, so I was sinking fast until I learned that planning and journaling, by doing this It created peace for me that's what it became A Mindful Existence

Since I do not want anyone to go through this and it might happen, or it could be happening to you right now .. I'm sharing. I want you to create your world of peace.

## A MINDFUL EXISTENCE

mind·ful
ˈmīn(d)fəl/
adjective
conscious or aware of something.
"we can be more mindful of the energy we use to heat our homes"
synonyms:    aware, conscious, sensible, alive, alert, acquainted, heedful, wary, chary; More

So here it is: When you are creating your business prepare it for the lifestyle that you want to have. Then plan around your current lifestyle.

Here's an example.
Entrepreneur A... let's call her Mary. Mary wants to travel extensively.

She doesn't want a large lawn, but would love a great view. She doesn't want anything but a goldfish as her pet. She currently has no support at home for babysitting, and her finances are limited. Mary probably shouldn't open a retail store in the Mall. Mary might find it very overwhelming as mall hours are long, and daycare is expensive. There is personnel that would need to be paid, and she needs to consider if the current business would sustain her when she travels.

When living a mindful existence you will recognize it as the key to dealing with relationships, selling, organization and even marketing. You will plan, and when so called obstacles come your way your understanding of the other factors might become clearer.

- So we will go over looking and understand ourselves
- Creating our goals and the keys to planning
- Overcoming obstacles and objection
- Creating our world of peace
- Sharing the peace

And yes you are going to write in this book. You will study and include your words it is Key to creating your world of peace.

## Chapter 2: Your World

Get your pen, and remember, I'm not going to read it; this is your journey! You need to think of your future when creating your business, so the space below is for you to write where/what you want to be. Yes, wealthy is an answer, but what do you envision once you are there: will you live here or abroad? Will you have pets? Will you have children? This will help in creating your dream.

You can continue this in a journal, and it might change. As you and your plan evolve regularly revisit your plans personal and business

## THE RIGHT NOW

So we look at all aspects of the planning ~ visions. And it looks great, our plans(I'm not sure you told them to plan it was more what is your goal) cannot fail...right? Well if I talk to people about their planning stages, of them wouldn't even have thought about their current lifestyles. Your business is your baby, but not an actual baby! It should fit into your current lifestyle and evolve as you do. The point of getting into business is not to feel burdened, until you despise it, and become so overwhelmed that you freeze in place. You need to first determine your WHY. Why plan this baby? Will it fit my current world?. The answer is not just money family, etc. you can do that with a 9-5, but the true reason inside yourself. Try using this space to write down your why, without using the old standby of family and wealth.

Now really think about your current lifestyle, does it fit into what you visualize for your business? Think about the people that you have around you; remember that having a mindful existence is more than just thinking about yourself. Your family has thoughts feelings etc. think about them in your decision process. Then talk to them, these people who play an important role in your dream, and whether you want to admit it or not, people can contribute to you decisions. Just remember negativity is not tolerated. But understand constructive criticism and be mindful of their concerns,

## Chapter 3: Recognizing Your Gift

Now, it may be that you have many gifts. And you could be jack-of-all-trades, and you can make some make jack-of-all trades money. But what we want is to become is a master. We all know a master or heard of them. We look up to them. We seek to learn from them. You want to be the master of your business, your product, or brand. You want to make master money. It helps if you do this by recognizing your gift and if the gift is your passion.

> "You must immerse yourself in your work. You have to fall in love with your work ... You must dedicate your life to mastering your skill. That's the secret of success."
> — Chef Jiro

Well you don't want to confuse your customer and want to build a culture based around your brand, and I know this sounds odd, but which one of your gifts is your passion?  Here are two examples:

I always heard I cut hair well (don't think I liked doing it that much).  I never went to expand my education; never voluntarily cut someone's hair etc.  I did open a salon once, but I rented out the booths.  That was not very lucrative or fulfilling.

I heard of a chocolate salesperson who was an introvert and loved creating beautiful chocolate creations.  He was not very assertive and used the creations as a hobby or to show the great candy he sold He was asked about his creations and found out that more of the stores were interested in his creations then his ingredients.  His clients never really paid attention to his scripted speech as much as this wonderful artisans work they wanted to carry in their shops.  He built a website, started to sell his creations wholesale; started a blog; and even started making videos on how to make some of this.  People could purchase the ingredients on his site or buy ready-made in local shops.  Now he is doing what he is passionate about and also created multiple streams of income.

To not share your gifts in my opinion is a sin, so how do we recognize our gifts?

I used to think that if a talent was not from the stage, screen, or a gallery then you had no talent.  That is not true!  Some of us work with our hands, some of us are great teachers, some of us are quite detailed, awesome chefs, seamstress etc.

Do this experiment:
Step back and think out of everything I do in this world what am I good at doing?  Ask the person you trust the most in the world if you do not already know.  I don't care if it's making chili!  You can make it and sell it.  You just have to research how.

## YOUR FAULTS

We would love to think that we don't have weaknesses or faults. However, I believe that we may have some traits that are not conducive to having a business. So the best way of dealing with it is to know and understand weaknesses.
So here are some things to consider: are you the procrastinator?
The king or queen of excuses? There's always a reason why you don't make a decision? Are you a fault finder?. Or do you say to yourself it has to be perfect? Are you the maximizer or minimizer while you are minimizing the benefits, you'll find that both of them kills your motivation.

If you think, "This project is too hard; I'll never get it done." you may be a magnifier and minimizer, making the more challenging aspects of a job way worse. Instead, say "This is a challenge, but it's doable, and the rewards of even getting started are well worth it."

If you think, "I could never do this on my own," or "I'm just never good at this kind of thing," you're likely a personalizer or over-generalizer, which points to low self-esteem. Because you don't believe you are capable of doing it, and you tell yourself that, well, you believe it, and your fear becomes your reality. Instead, say, "What I'm attempting to do wouldn't be easy for anyone. Who better than me to take it on? Who else but me is even willing to take it on?"

If you think, "Nothing ever works out for me," or "I don't have what it takes to get this done," then you have a self-defeating explanatory style. You see situations as unchangeable, and if you believe that, well, you can see why you wouldn't bother attempting to do anything. Instead, say, "Every project, no matter how big, has a beginning, and this is it." Find one part of the project you know you're good at and start there.

Are you a space cadet? You dream and it's far out or you act on it with no planning.

Write them down, your faults on a separate sheet of paper. Then think of ways to get around these faults when they rear their ugly heads. So if you are a space cadet plan, plan, plan. If you are a fault-finder right down positive words of affirmation, and if excuses are your what stops you then answer those excuses with the positive reason to proceed.

There are so many more faults, and we can have several, We need to develop ways to deal with them. Then, if you remember to pick a business that suits your passions and lifestyle for now, and what you want your lifestyle to be in the future, your faults are not so much of an obstacle

**What are your gifts? In the space provided jot down your gifts. Then next to that think of ways you can make money with those gifts.**

If you need more space write it on a separate paper

## CHAPTER 4: PROCRASTINATION

pro·cras·ti·na·tion

prə͵krastə'nāSH(ə)n/
noun
the action of delaying or postponing something.
"Your first tip is to avoid procrastination,"

Most of you know the definition; we even know when we are in the midst of it. We sometimes laugh at it, and we kick ourselves after time has past. How can we deal with this very difficult habit? Telling you to plan ~ will it help if you won't even grab your planner. So let's review a few things. There is good procrastination, you are doing way too much and your body and mind are saying rest. However procrastination works as a virus and will attach itself to the things that you need to do.

We will review planning later, but one of the things that we see happens is what we *think* has a profound effect on what we *do*--even whether or not we put things off. Negative emotions are caused by negative thoughts that derail your ability to get things done, because faced with the thing you should do (clean the garage, write the proposal, apply for the job), you are so daunted or intimidated or tired that you'll revert instead to tasks that you want to do--the feel-good activities (check Facebook, watch TV, lie down)--assuming you'll feel better later to tackle the hard thing ~ except this doesn't happen. You feel worse after having put it off!

We need to shift our brain from me-focused thinking and promote mindful and positive thinking.

Here's how to start redirecting your energy from mood-fixing, goal-derailing activities and get yourself back on track.

## 1. Find the ground wire

ground wire
nounNORTH AMERICAN
a wire that has an electrical connection to the earth, either directly or through another grounded conductor.
"check the ground wire and connection"

First, you have to understand and identify what you're trying to do and what is holding you back. Identify the cause of that overwhelming feeling. What are the thoughts that creep up when you attempt to write the proposal or have a difficult conversation? What do you fear could happen if you actually do it? What's the worst-case scenario? For many, if not most, anxiety is to blame. The anxiety of messing up the job, or not getting it done, leads us to put it off until, ironically, we can't get it done well or done at all:

## 2. Reward Instead of Avoid

I f your mood plummets at the prospect of taking action, then include a reward system in your plan. Set the timer and for every 15 minutes of uninterrupted paperwork, you get to turn up the music and dance. You can look in the mirror and speak words of affirmation as the goal is to heal your mood first. This is how you end up in the social media whirlpool. Instead, tell yourself that doing something, anything, will yield a reward--later. Think of it as procrastinating the fun stuff.

## 3. Watch for the Brickwall

You have a whole bunch of ideas about how the world works and should work that have gradually formed in your head, beginning when you were very young, but you're barely aware of them, since they've sunk below the surface of your consciousness. These I'll call Brickwall Beliefs, and they can be a problem because you're likely unaware of how they are affecting your thinking. One example of a Brickwall Belief at play with procrastination is, "I need everything perfect." (Sound familiar?). This need to have things a certain way before you take any action will delay your progress and you might not get anything done. How do you know you're dealing with a brickwall? The signs include words such as "I should" or "I must" keep spinning through your mind.

## 4. Work on you Mindful Existence

The way you perceive a situation will determine how you respond to it--and ultimately, what you do. What happens to many of us is that we get stuck in a thinking quicksand. How do you get out of quicksand? You're hiking alone in the wilderness, lost in your thoughts, when suddenly you find yourself trapped in quicksand and sinking fast. Is it a certain muddy death? It doesn't have to be. Here's what to do if you find yourself with that sinking feeling, or if you are thinking in a way that leaves us no way out or forward: even if you are alone put the word *we* on your mind. Think it through as if you have a team that will help you tackle the project, and the team will celebrate later. Put positive thoughts into effect until you feel like a corny Valentine's Day card. Positive thinking will have positive results; having a positive result should be rewarded

## 5. Reframe It

The pain of doing a tough thing now pales in comparison to the pain of regret later if you didn't even try. Ask yourself, what do you stand to lose by not doing it? How will your life, your career, your relationships suffer as a result of inaction? If there's no dire reason or no consequence why let it take up your time. Tell yourself that it's not just about how difficult the task is -- it's about putting real effort into something you care about. Just do these things that must be done. (We call these weeds and seeds we will review later.) And I promise you, there's no better reward than that. So next time you find yourself putting off a major task, find the root of the problem; shift your thinking; and reframe your thinking. You'll find yourself checking things off your to-do list, and enjoying down time much more.

## Chapter 5: Stepping out on faith

" Faith is taking the first step even if you don't see the whole staircase."
~ Martin Luther king Jr

I am not giving you a sermon as much as talking to you about dealing with negativity and working with the positive. You have stepped out on faith in yourself or your product or capabilities, and for that you need to reward yourself. However, once you share your ideas with others they might not share your dreams. Which is ok, **you** were given the dream not them. Share the gift with everyone however the dream in the beginning should be shared selectively from the start, and here's why not everyone will have your best interest in mind or they will be negative due to fear or personality
Learning to Recognizing these people in your life gives you the advantage and keeping positive people in your life who will nurture your dream and help it grow.

**The Skunks** are people who always see what's bad with everything and everyone else but can't see what's wrong in their lives. They are negative from the start and you can smell them coming from miles away

**The Raccoons** listen to your ideas then make it theirs so protect your products and or ideas legally, get your trademarks you patents, This is why your business attorneys will be worth having in the very beginning; do not give information to people that do not deserve it!

**The Green eyed Hawks** have nothing but envy in their hearts. They will act as if they have your back but they secretly envy you; to me they are the most dangerous. Just count on your listening skills when you are talking about your business or dreams as they're very passive aggressive. They might give positive lip service but negative or no action. The passive aggressive

pas·sive-ag·gres·sive
adjective
of or denoting a type of behavior or personality characterized by indirect resistance to the demands of others and an avoidance of direct confrontation, as in procrastinating, pouting, or misplacing important materials.

**The Exotic Pets** want a lot of our time. usually give into them, but other than babies and underage children, they're at the point where they can take care of themselves. They are sometimes significant others and . they can also be friends; these are the thieves of our time. Always remember time is money. They are emotionally greedy

How do we deal with these people? Know them for what they are and keep these letters in mind **S.S.M.**
**S** = See. Recognize them for what they are.
**S** = Speak. Think of yourself as a star and they are the press. Give them a smile and a little conversation, or avoid them if they are really caustic.
**M**= Move Keep it short as the more you speak the more they are taking your money. Don't help a thief take your money (time).

Now we will focus on the positive people that will help us on our road to success. They might not even understand the why, the how, but because it's you they support you 100 percent in various ways

You Accountant should be one of the first people you seek. Get referrals.
Your Attorney. Specifically one who specializes in small business. He or she will help you set up your business and any patents or trademarks to protect yourself and your intellectual property.

Keep people around, especially other entrepreneurs, and find allies outside your direct community. You want to build a tribe around your brand, yourself, and your dream. Invest in a coach if you need to do so; however, make sure you have clear expectations and a contract to ensure your needs are met.

# FEAR

Sometimes when you're in a dark place, you think you've been buried,
but you've actually been planted
~ By The Unbound Spirit

As I was writing this, my business bestie sent this to me, and I thought how fitting. right?

Fear is going to rear its ugly head at any moment. As it happens we must be able to deal with it because it's a form of doubt and doubt has no place in faith and dealing with it.

Avoiding what we are afraid of prevents us from moving forward—it makes us anxious. Therapists can be invaluable in helping us work through our avoiding strategies. If you have experienced trauma, it is especially important to work with a therapist to create a safe environment where you can face your fear and reconstruct your memories.

So here are some techniques for mild occasions.

"Every time your fear is invited up, every time you recognize it and smile at it, your fear will lose some of its strength."
~ Thich Nhat Hanh

- **Mindful Meditation -** Go to the a quiet place; feel the fear, and as it creeps in your body, gently and slowly, start breathing it out of your body,
- **Develop a plan** - A healthy lifestyle promoting self-control is great.
    The serenity prayer helps with this.
    God, grant me the serenity to accept the
    things I cannot change,
    The courage to change the things I can,

And wisdom to know the difference
This classic is still the best.

**Promote positivity** - Once everyone you know understands that negativity is not tolerated, it will not only weed out the skunks in your life but attract more positive thinkers as friends and positive thinking on your part. According to research by Barbara Fredrickson, positivity broadens our perspective—we literally have a wider view, which offers us more options. And the more we practice positivity, the more it builds, creating a resilience that allows us to function even in difficult times.

**Learn the reason why =** If something happens to you, fear can shatter the world as we know it. And your business can suffer, Having systems in place for the worst scenario helps keep the business running as you. seek help. Finding a sense of purpose of security and professional will help in this journey.

Practice stress reduction techniques such as mindfulness meditation or aerobic exercise.
Shift your focus to the positive emotions in daily life.
Work to identify daily meaning and purpose .
Get support from others.
Go for a walk or run in a park.
There are many tips and tricks of the trade, but the main thing is that you did it. You stepped out on faith! You know what you want and are ready to get out there and be the conqueror. You need to develop now smarter goals

# Chapter 6: Smarter Goals

Nothing that I'm telling you is rocket science. Make an annual vision plan for your business. Break up your goals in increments of 90 days. This is where a system needs to kick in gear, and you add to your lifestyle habits what will be the key to your success.

So let's go over smart goals

**S.M.A.R.T.E.R** remember these letters

**Specific** Does your goal clearly and specifically state what you are trying to achieve? If your goal is particularly lofty, try breaking it down into smaller specific goals. Why is this so important? Well, in goal setting, in order to make it visceral to the mind and more clear, you have to be able to quantify that goal. Without specifics, there's no real target, just some obscure direction. When the goal is obscure, it allows the psychology of your mind to override your goals. You succumb to emotion-numbing activities to easily avoid doing something that wasn't that concrete in the first place.

Specifics are the fuel in the engine of your goals. You have to provide specifics if you're going to achieve anything. When you write out your goals, be absolutely as specific as possible. And never be afraid to be too specific.

Write down a specific goal.

**Meaningful/Measurable** How will you see if progress is being made? Can you quantify or put numbers to your outcome? When your goals have a deep enough meaning to you, you'll do whatever it takes to achieve them. This doesn't have to do with vanity or superficial reasons, but more profound and life-altering reasons why you want to achieve something.

Looking at the goal you wrote in the space provided above,

**Attainable** Who else is in the picture? Do you have factors that prevent you from accomplishing your goals and can it be reframed. Set goals that you can actually achieve so that you build on your momentum. Your short-term goals should be something within your reach, but not so easily attainable that they won't take much work or effort on your part. This will also help you build that all-important momentum. Once you achieve your year-long goals, you can broaden those into much greater hopes and dreams down the road.

Is the goal you wrote previously attainable? What are the steps to make it happen?

Who are the main players?




**Relevant** This is your why; why are you doing this? What effect will this create for others? When you set goals that are relevant, you have to dig deep down inside and truly understand what you want out of life. If one of your core values is freedom, then setting goals that have you bound to a desk most of the year won't help you to live a fulfilled life. Remember, your goals shouldn't be designed with the notion of succeeding to be happy, but rather, with happily succeeding. Set goals that are relevant and in line with what you truly want out of life.

What is the why in the goal you previously recorded?



**Time-bound** Give a date. When will you reach the goal. If the goal is large break it up into smaller goals. When your goals are time-bound, they're measurable, and you should hold yourself accountable by measuring those goals on a daily, weekly, and monthly basis. How close are you to achieving your goals? How much further did you get from achieving your goals? Without making your goals time-bound and measurable, you won't be able to see your progress

When will this goal be completed? Give it a date.

**Evalute** By evaluating your goals every single day, you'll be much more likely to achieve them. Why is that? Well, long-term goals (and also goals that are 3 months or 6 months out), can easily be ignored if they aren't evaluated every single day.Make sure that you set up a system for evaluating your goals and you make the evaluation of your goals habitual. Don't ignore this all-important step. Your mind has a very clever way of allowing you to ignore your goals by pushing you into emotion-numbing behaviors when those goals aren't closely evaluated.

Evaluate the goal daily? What might need to change?
You will use this as a section in your journal.

**Reward** Recognition of your achievements should bring a reward. Work hard, play hard should not just be a saying at the end of your goal - add a reward. You deserve it, and it will be useful for fuel, as you are working on your goals.

What is your reward to yourself? (Write It)

## Chapter 7 Planning

Planning or journaling

Creating a weekly plan will help you achieve these goals by creating smart actions daily. Think of using your smart goals daily
There is not a time of day that I can recommend for you to brain release. A brain release is when you take 3-5 minutes and write down all that is on your mind, reflect and prioritize. But it will start with remembering a goal. So we can start with understanding goals and the difference with the steps to achieve it.

An example we will use is Michael. Michael decided to start a business catering from home; his goal is to be up and running in 90 days. Michael does have a business plan, but his day-to-day needs to be considered so he created a pyramid on a poster board. On the top he wrote opening day and the date and the rest of the pyramid is in months. He writes what he has to do and gives each item dates. All the dates lead up to that opening date thus giving him a visual.

But let's talk day-to-day. Are you a morning person, afternoon or night?. What is the quietest time of day?. Some people get up 7am they have a thousand things on their mind so they get the coffee brewing and they don't have to open the store till 10am. So this is a great time to open the planner and get everything off their mind. For some the day is hectic, however, they cannot sleep at night. So preparing the Daily Plan is a great way to decompress and a brain release is optimum at this time.

So what I'm saying is take your planner; make a section in which to release. You can call it the dumping ground, transfer station, or even deposits. Whatever makes you remember to clear your head on paper. Now look at it; what can you honestly do that day and section those things into categories. I'm going to give you examples you can call them whatever works for you.

I would start out using a black planner or composition book. Get Colored pencils or Post It notes, and do this daily.

## EARTH

These are the things that you must do this as a foundation of the day. It starts with reviewing your goal; it can also determine your day. Always keeping in mind the goal at the end of 90 days, give the item a star or something next to it that shows it's important. After it has been achieved remember to reward yourself. It is also your schedule so look at how much time you should put to each task and stick to it. For example if someone calls you understand it's not an emergency and they are stealing time from you. Schedule everything!

What is your 90 day goal.? Why is this here?

## YOUR SPRINKLER SYSTEM

Take everything out of your mind and put it on paper. It doesn't have to be about business only just let it flow unto the paper. And then pick out the things you need to do for the day the best time of the day in which to do it. This is the beginning of your to-do list, and even that should have categories.

Get it off your mind, and onto paper.

## YOUR GARDEN TOOLS

These are your accountability partners, your delegates, the tribe that will contribute to your success. It includes your attorney, your accountant, your financial planner friends and family etc.

Who are your accountability partners and other delegates?




## SEEDS

These are the things we do that we know must result in a crop or flowers. It can be sales calls, writing in Blog, working on your press release, or creating a event. If you have ever worked on a garden then you know not every seed flourishes and not everyone will say Yes! however only give those be it rejection etc. one minute . Then resume The more seeds you plant the crop you'll gather.

Who do you need to call? Attend networking events? How many proposals?

## PRUNING

This is the necessary things you do for your business that you might not necessarily like doing. For some it could be working on numbers or your website, but it will not be a healthy business if these things are not done. If it's not pruned or weeded it will creates a mess. Pruning is doing what we least like to do, what we will probably procrastinate on, but it is necessary so get it out of the way.

Write down three things you don't really want to do but must do

1.

2.

3.

## THE VASE

What I notice more than anything is that we do not reward ourselves, there is a Place in our head that we work for free because it's our own business.. that's crazy! We need to reward ourselves for our hard work. So pat yourselves on the back; write down your successes. Think of it as bringing the fresh flowers home and putting them in a vase on your table. .

What's your reward for hard work? Every day you hit your goals treat yourself.

The one we really keep forgetting ...
Now when you keep pushing a task week after week put it on the back burner or hire someone to do it. Wasting time on a task is wasting money.

These are the ways I break up my days. You can name them whatever makes sense to you. But for this book I'll just keep referring to My Garden. I want my business to grow.

## HABITS

Creating this into habit means remembering to actually do the work. well set a time to do this it will take 3-5 minutes a day. It will continue to be what manifests your vision.

This routine will be the first steps to Mindful Existence. This is the planning and we will look at overcoming obstacles that will happen even with the best laid out plans.

In the next few pages you will start journaling, start cleansing and writing.

1. What are your desires for your company?
2. How do you picture yourself during retirement?
3. Take note of how the people around you react to your new or current business.
4. Take note of your fears and visualize ways to decrease anxiety.

I know some people hate a book with blank pages, however, this is a book I want you to carry around and use as a reference. Use colored pens or pencils, Post-It notes, or whatever makes this yours.
Color code a system that will make you understand the importance of your tasks, Or put boxes, check marks or stars to create a key to what is finished, incomplete or yet to be started.

Your journal

## WRITE YOUR SMARTER GOAL
## (THE EARTH)

Please write down you 90-day goal(s). (Remember S.M.A.R.T.E.R )

Record your Accomplishment Key. This is the method for which you will track your progress. Write your color codes example black is done, red in incomplete yellow means not attempted, or your symbols: a check is completed, and an arrow means moved forward..

# Day 1

**Sprinkler System.** Write your daily thoughts.

**Garden Tools.** Your delegates

**Pruning.** Write what you must do but really don't want to do.

**Seeds** are the sales pitches, business calls, proposals, etc

**The vase** how you will celebrate or reward yourself.

# Day 2

**Your sprinklers system** write your daily thoughts

**Your Garden tools** your delegates

**Pruning** write what you must do but really don't want to

**Seeds** these are the sales pitches, business calls, proposals, etc

**The vase**

# Day 3

**Your sprinklers system** write your daily thoughts

**Your Garden tools** your delegates

**Pruning** write what you must do but really don't want to




**Seeds** these are the sales pitches, business calls, proposals, etc




**The vase**

# Day 4

**Your sprinklers system** write your daily thoughts

**Your Garden tools** your delegates

**Pruning** write what you must do but really don't want to

**Seeds** these are the sales pitches, business calls, proposals, etc

**The vase**

# Day 5

**Your sprinklers system** write your daily thoughts

**Your Garden tools** your delegates

**Pruning** write what you must do but really don't want to

**Seeds** these are the sales pitches, business calls, proposals, etc

**The vase**

# Day 6

**Your sprinklers system** write your daily thoughts

**Your Garden tools** your delegates

**Pruning** write what you must do but really don't want to

**Seeds** these are the sales pitches, business calls, proposals, etc

**The vase**

# Day 7

**Your sprinklers system** write your daily thoughts

**Your Garden tools** your delegates

**Pruning** write what you must do but really don't want to

**Seeds** these are the sales pitches, business calls, proposals, etc

**The vase**

## Day 8

**Your sprinklers system** write your daily thoughts

**Your Garden tools** your delegates

**Pruning** write what you must do but really don't want to

**Seeds** these are the sales pitches, business calls, proposals, etc

**The vase**

# Day 9

**Your sprinklers system** write your daily thoughts

**Your Garden tools** your delegates




**Pruning** write what you must do but really don't want to




**Seeds** these are the sales pitches, business calls, proposals, etc

**The vase**

# Day 10

**Your sprinklers system** write your daily thoughts

**Your Garden tools** your delegates

**Pruning** write what you must do but really don't want to

**Seeds** these are the sales pitches, business calls, proposals, etc

**The vase**

# Day 11

**Your sprinklers system** write your daily thoughts

**Your Garden tools** your delegates

**Pruning** write what you must do but really don't want to

**Seeds** these are the sales pitches, business calls, proposals, etc

**The vase**

## Day 12

**Your sprinklers system** write your daily thoughts

**Your Garden tools** your delegates

**Pruning** write what you must do but really don't want to

**Seeds** these are the sales pitches, business calls, proposals, etc

**The vase**

# Day 13

**Your sprinklers system** write your daily thoughts

**Your Garden tools** your delegates




**Pruning** write what you must do but really don't want to




**Seeds** these are the sales pitches, business calls, proposals, etc

**The vase**

## Day 14

**Your sprinklers system** write your daily thoughts

**Your Garden tools** your delegates

**Pruning** write what you must do but really don't want to

**Seeds** these are the sales pitches, business calls, proposals, etc

**The vase**

# Day 15

**Your sprinklers system** write your daily thoughts

**Your Garden tools** your delegates




**Pruning** write what you must do but really don't want to








**Seeds** these are the sales pitches, business calls, proposals, etc

**The vase**

## Day 16

**Your sprinklers system** write your daily thoughts

**Your Garden tools** your delegates

**Pruning** write what you must do but really don't want to

**Seeds** these are the sales pitches, business calls, proposals, etc

**The vase**

# Day 17

**Your sprinklers system** write your daily thoughts

**Your Garden tools** your delegates




**Pruning** write what you must do but really don't want to




**Seeds** these are the sales pitches, business calls, proposals, etc

The vase


# Day 18


**Your sprinklers system** write your daily thoughts




**Your Garden tools** your delegates




**Pruning** write what you must do but really don't want to

**Seeds** these are the sales pitches, business calls, proposals, etc

The vase

# Day 19

**Your sprinklers system** write your daily thoughts

**Your Garden tools** your delegates




**Pruning** write what you must do but really don't want to




**Seeds** these are the sales pitches, business calls, proposals, etc

The vase

## Day 20

**Your sprinklers system** write your daily thoughts

**Your Garden tools** your delegates

**Pruning** write what you must do but really don't want to

**Seeds** these are the sales pitches, business calls, proposals, etc

**The vase**

# Day 21

**Your sprinklers system** write your daily thoughts

**Your Garden tools** your delegates

**Pruning** write what you must do but really don't want to

**Seeds** these are the sales pitches, business calls, proposals, etc

The vase

# Day 22

**Your sprinklers system** write your daily thoughts

**Your Garden tools** your delegates

**Pruning** write what you must do but really don't want to

**Seeds** these are the sales pitches, business calls, proposals, etc

**The vase**

# Day 23

**Your sprinklers system** write your daily thoughts

**Your Garden tools** your delegates




**Pruning** write what you must do but really don't want to




**Seeds** these are the sales pitches, business calls, proposals, etc

The vase

## Day 24

**Your sprinklers system** write your daily thoughts




**Your Garden tools** your delegates




**Pruning** write what you must do but really don't want to

**Seeds** these are the sales pitches, business calls, proposals, etc

**The vase**

# Day 25

**Your sprinklers system** write your daily thoughts

**Your Garden tools** your delegates

**Pruning** write what you must do but really don't want to

**Seeds** these are the sales pitches, business calls, proposals, etc

The vase

# Day 26

**Your sprinklers system** write your daily thoughts

**Your Garden tools** your delegates

**Pruning** write what you must do but really don't want to

**Seeds** these are the sales pitches, business calls, proposals, etc

The vase

# Day 27

**Your sprinklers system** write your daily thoughts

**Your Garden tools** your delegates




**Pruning** write what you must do but really don't want to




**Seeds** these are the sales pitches, business calls, proposals, etc

**The vase**

## Day 28

**Your sprinklers system** write your daily thoughts

**Your Garden tools** your delegates

**Pruning** write what you must do but really don't want to

**Seeds** these are the sales pitches, business calls, proposals, etc

**The vase**

# Day 29

**Your sprinklers system** write your daily thoughts

**Your Garden tools** your delegates

**Pruning** write what you must do but really don't want to

**Seeds** these are the sales pitches, business calls, proposals, etc

The vase

## Day 30

**Your sprinklers system** write your daily thoughts

**Your Garden tools** your delegates

**Pruning** write what you must do but really don't want to

**Seeds** these are the sales pitches, business calls, proposals, etc

The vase

# Day 31

**Your sprinklers system** write your daily thoughts

**Your Garden tools** your delegates




**Pruning** write what you must do but really don't want to




**Seeds** these are the sales pitches, business calls, proposals, etc

**The vase**

"Give me six hours to chop down a tree and I will spend the first four sharpening the axe."
— Abraham Lincoln

## ABOUT THE AUTHOR

Ellice Darien lives In chesterfield Virginia has 3 children and 1 grandson  she is the owner of ByDarien LLC
[Www.bydarien.com](Www.bydarien.com)

She runs various workshops geared to the entrepreneur and also teaches soapmaking and better ways to sell her products with ByDarien representatives

www.ingramcontent.com/pod-product-compliance
Lightning Source LLC
Chambersburg PA
CBHW070108210526
45170CB00013B/794